Learn to Fold Origami
Dinosaurs

Katie Gillespie

www.av2books.com

AV² provides enriched content that supplements and complements this book. Weigl's AV² books strive to create inspired learning and engage young minds in a total learning experience.

Your AV² Media Enhanced books come alive with...

Audio
Listen to sections of the book read aloud.

Key Words
Study vocabulary, and complete a matching word activity.

Video
Watch informative video clips.

Quizzes
Test your knowledge.

Go to **www.av2books.com**, and enter this book's unique code.

BOOK CODE

J268596

Embedded Weblinks
Gain additional information for research.

Slide Show
View images and captions, and prepare a presentation.

AV² by Weigl brings you media enhanced books that support active learning.

Try This!
Complete activities and hands-on experiments.

... and much, much more!

Published by AV² by Weigl
350 5th Avenue, 59th Floor
New York, NY 10118
Website: www.weigl.com   www.av2books.com

Library of Congress Control Number: 2013939642

ISBN 978-1-62127-676-0 (hardcover)
ISBN 978-1-62127-677-7 (softcover)
ISBN 978-1-62127-780-4 (single user eBook)
ISBN 978-1-48960-031-8 (multi-user eBook)

Printed in the United States of America in North Mankato, Minnesota
1 2 3 4 5 6 7 8 9 0   17 16 15 14 13

062013
WEP220513

Senior Editor: Heather Kissock
Art Director: Terry Paulhus

Every reasonable effort has been made to trace ownership and to obtain permission to reprint copyright material. The publishers would be pleased to have any errors or omissions brought to their attention so that they may be corrected in subsequent printings.

Weigl acknowledges Getty Images as its primary image supplier for this title.

Origami patterns adapted from concepts originating with Fumiaki Shingu.

2

Contents

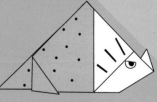

Why Fold Origami?

Origami is the Japanese art of paper folding. The Japanese, and the Chinese before them, have been folding paper into different shapes and designs for hundreds of years. The term "origami" comes from the Japanese words "ori," which means "folding," and "kami," which means "paper."

Paper used to be very expensive, so origami was an activity that only the rich could afford. Over time, paper became less expensive, and more people were able to participate in origami. Today, it is an art form that anyone can enjoy.

It is fun to make objects out of paper. Before you start doing origami, there are three basic folds that you must learn. Knowing these three folds will help you create almost any simple origami model.

Hood Fold

Hood folds are often used to make an animal's head or neck. To make a hood fold, fold along the dotted line, and crease. Then, unfold the paper. Open the pocket you have created. Flip the paper inside out along the creases, and flatten.

Pocket Fold

Pocket folds are often used to make an animal's mouth or tail. To make a pocket fold, fold along the dotted line, and crease. Then, unfold the paper. Open the pocket you have created. Fold the point inside along the creases, and flatten.

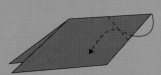

Step Fold

Step folds are often used to make an animal's ears. To make a step fold, fold backward along the dotted line, and crease. Then, fold frontward along the dotted line, and crease. Repeat as necessary.

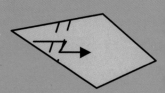

You will need:

- Origami paper (or any square-shaped paper)
- Colored markers or crayons

Practice making your favorite dinosaurs in this book to learn the skills needed to fold origami.

Dinosaurs

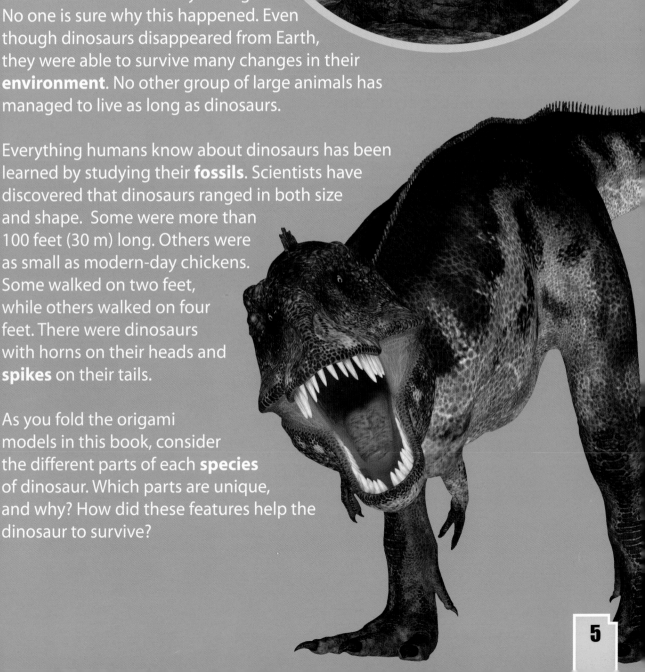

Long before humans lived, dinosaurs roamed Earth. They ruled the world for 160 million years. During this time, some dinosaurs became the biggest and strongest animals ever to walk on land. Dinosaurs became **extinct** about 65 million years ago. No one is sure why this happened. Even though dinosaurs disappeared from Earth, they were able to survive many changes in their **environment**. No other group of large animals has managed to live as long as dinosaurs.

Everything humans know about dinosaurs has been learned by studying their **fossils**. Scientists have discovered that dinosaurs ranged in both size and shape. Some were more than 100 feet (30 m) long. Others were as small as modern-day chickens. Some walked on two feet, while others walked on four feet. There were dinosaurs with horns on their heads and **spikes** on their tails.

As you fold the origami models in this book, consider the different parts of each **species** of dinosaur. Which parts are unique, and why? How did these features help the dinosaur to survive?

What Is a Brachiosaurus?

The brachiosaurus is one of the largest dinosaurs ever discovered. It stood about 40 feet (12 m) tall and could be up to 85 feet (26 m) long. A brachiosaurus could weigh up to 88 tons (80,000 kg).

Brachiosauruses were **herbivores**. They needed to eat up to 500 pounds (227 kg) of leaves and other plants each day to survive. Their height allowed them to eat the tops of tall trees that other dinosaurs could not reach.

The name "brachiosaurus" is Greek for "arm lizard." It was given this name because it had longer front legs than back legs.

Nose

The brachiosaurus had a very small head when compared to the rest of its body. A dome-shaped ridge on top of the head contained the animal's nostrils. A brachiosaurus's nostrils were quite large. The brachiosaurus likely had a good sense of smell.

Feet

A brachiosaurus had four feet. Each foot had five toes. Two toes on each front foot had claws. Each back foot had three clawed toes.

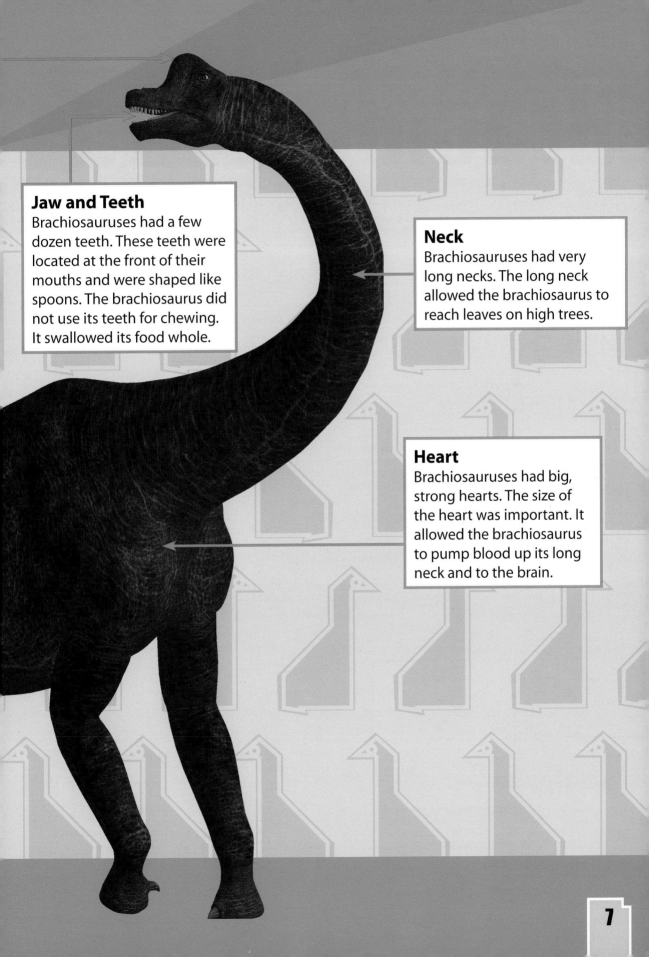

Jaw and Teeth
Brachiosauruses had a few dozen teeth. These teeth were located at the front of their mouths and were shaped like spoons. The brachiosaurus did not use its teeth for chewing. It swallowed its food whole.

Neck
Brachiosauruses had very long necks. The long neck allowed the brachiosaurus to reach leaves on high trees.

Heart
Brachiosauruses had big, strong hearts. The size of the heart was important. It allowed the brachiosaurus to pump blood up its long neck and to the brain.

7

How to Fold a
Brachiosaurus

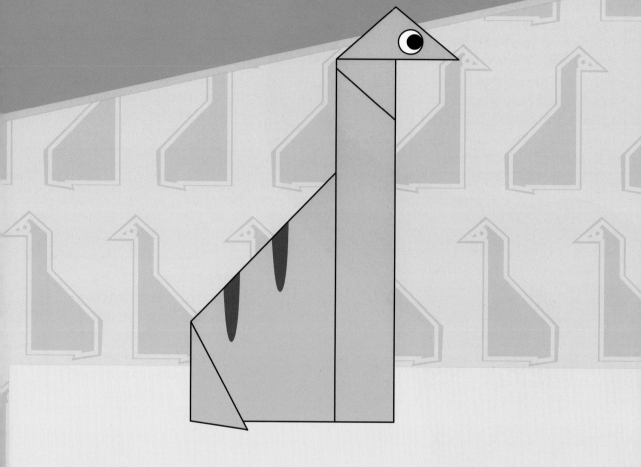

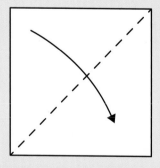

1 Fold in half, as shown.

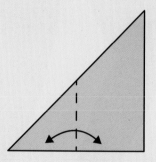

2 Fold the left point in along the dotted line, and crease. Open the paper.

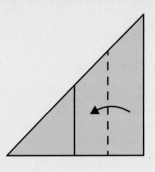

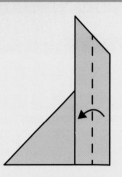

3 Fold the right side in along the dotted line, as shown.

4 Fold the right side in along the dotted line, as shown.

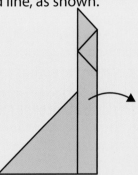

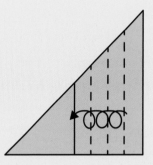

5 Open the paper.

6 Roll the right side of the paper toward the center line, as shown.

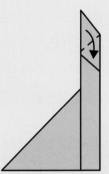

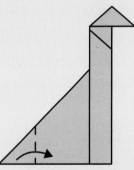

7 To make the brachiosaurus's head, fold the top point down along the dotted line.

8 Fold the left point in along the dotted line, as shown, to make the brachiosaurus's tail.

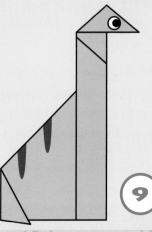

9 Finish the brachiosaurus by drawing its eye and pattern.

What Is an Iguanodon?

The iguanodon roamed Earth between 110 and 140 million years ago. It was an herbivore that ate ferns and other plants. The iguanodon was named for its teeth. The word "iguanodon" means "iguana tooth." An iguanodon's teeth looked like the teeth of a modern-day iguana.

Iguanodons stood about 16 feet (5 m) tall and ranged from 30 to 33 feet (9 to 10 m) in length. They weighed between 3.5 and 5 tons (4,000 and 5,000 kg). It is believed that iguanodons lived in herds. This is because many iguanodon fossils have been found in groups.

Tail

Iguanodons had long, flat tails that were carried high off the ground. The tail always remained straight and never bent. This helped the iguanodon keep its **balance** whether it was walking on two legs or four.

Legs

An iguanodon's back legs were much longer than its front legs. It could walk on two feet, but its stiff tail would not allow it to stand upright. The iguanodon could easily shift between walking on two legs and walking on four legs. These dinosaurs were relatively quick. They could run at speeds of up to 15 miles (24 km) per hour.

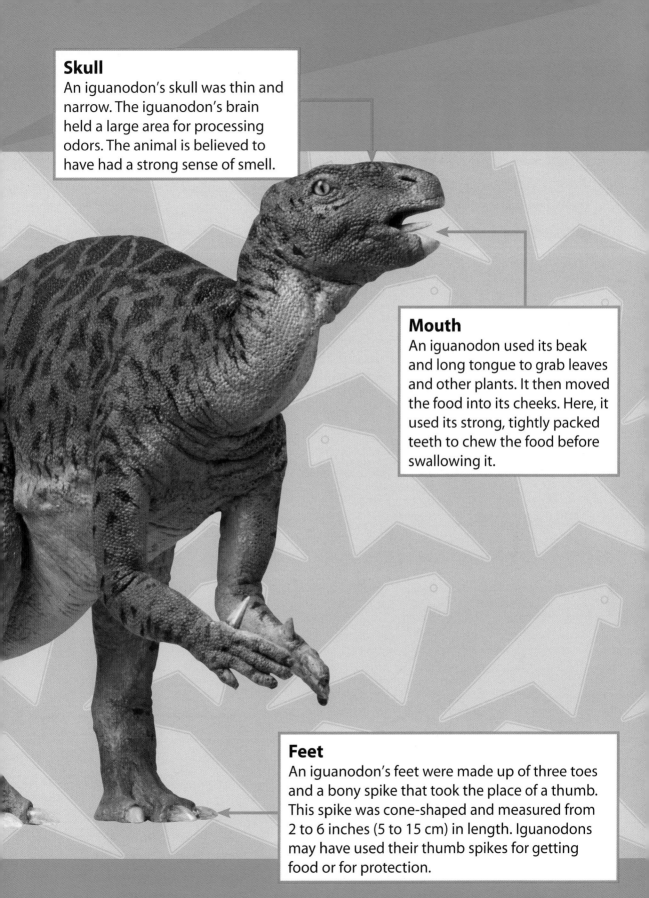

Skull
An iguanodon's skull was thin and narrow. The iguanodon's brain held a large area for processing odors. The animal is believed to have had a strong sense of smell.

Mouth
An iguanodon used its beak and long tongue to grab leaves and other plants. It then moved the food into its cheeks. Here, it used its strong, tightly packed teeth to chew the food before swallowing it.

Feet
An iguanodon's feet were made up of three toes and a bony spike that took the place of a thumb. This spike was cone-shaped and measured from 2 to 6 inches (5 to 15 cm) in length. Iguanodons may have used their thumb spikes for getting food or for protection.

How to Fold an
Iguanodon

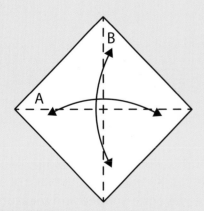

1 Fold in half along line A, and crease. Open the paper. Then, fold in half along line B, and crease. Open the paper.

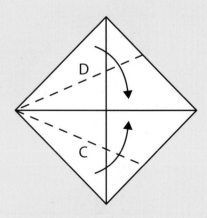

2 Fold up along line C to meet the center line, as shown. Then, fold down along line D to meet the center line.

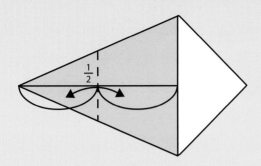

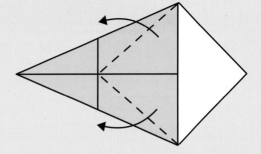

3 Fold in half along the dotted line, and crease. Then, fold back.

4 Fold the top flap along the dotted line. Repeat on the bottom flap.

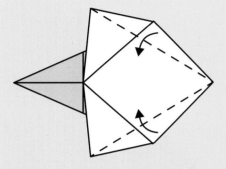

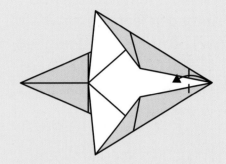

5 Fold the top in along the dotted line, as shown. Repeat on the bottom.

6 Fold the right point in along the dotted line.

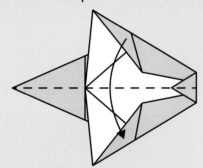

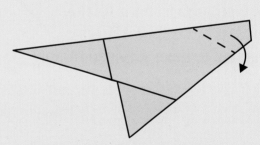

7 Fold in half lengthwise.

8 Turn the iguanodon around. To make the iguanodon's head, fold down along the dotted line.

9 Finish the iguanodon by drawing its eye and pattern.

What Is a Spinosaurus?

Spinosauruses were some of the largest **carnivorous** dinosaurs that ever existed. They ranged in length from 40 to 60 feet (12 to 18 m) and weighed up to 46,000 pounds (20,870 kg). Due to its size, the spinosaurus had few **predators**.

The spinosaurus lived in swamps and marshes. This allowed it to find food both on land and in water. Although it was large enough to hunt smaller dinosaurs, the spinosaurus is believed to have survived mainly on fish.

Legs
Scientists believe that the spinosaurus walked upright most of the time. Its muscular legs allowed it to reach speeds of up to 15 miles (24 km) per hour.

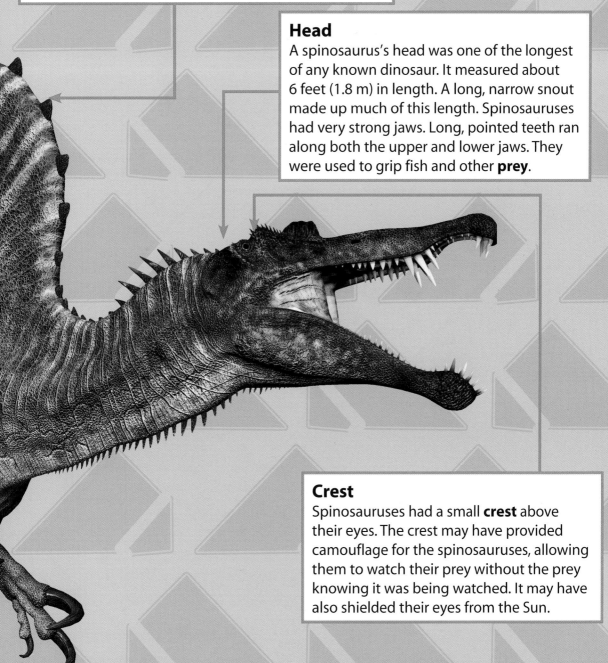

Sail

The name "spinosaurus" means "spiny lizard." This dinosaur was named for the long **spines** that ran along its back. Each spine was up to 6 feet (1.8 m) long. The spines came together to form the dinosaur's sail. Scientists believe the sail was used to attract **mates**, control **body temperature**, or possibly store water.

Head

A spinosaurus's head was one of the longest of any known dinosaur. It measured about 6 feet (1.8 m) in length. A long, narrow snout made up much of this length. Spinosauruses had very strong jaws. Long, pointed teeth ran along both the upper and lower jaws. They were used to grip fish and other **prey**.

Crest

Spinosauruses had a small **crest** above their eyes. The crest may have provided camouflage for the spinosauruses, allowing them to watch their prey without the prey knowing it was being watched. It may have also shielded their eyes from the Sun.

How to Fold a
Spinosaurus

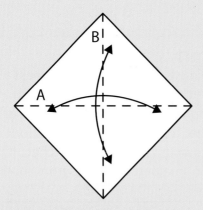

1 Fold in half along line A, and crease. Open the paper. Then, fold in half along line B, and crease. Open the paper.

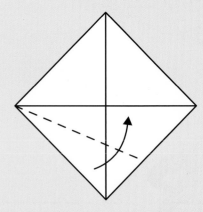

2 Fold the bottom point up along the dotted line to meet the center line.

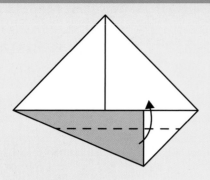

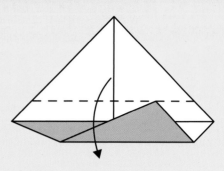

3 Fold the bottom up along the dotted line.

4 Fold the top point down along the dotted line.

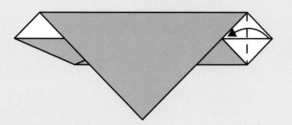

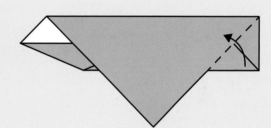

5 Fold the right point in along the dotted line.

6 Fold the right point up along the dotted line, as shown.

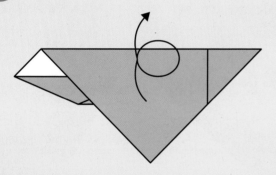

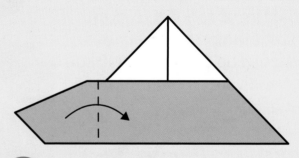

7 Turn the spinosaurus over.

8 Fold the left point in along the dotted line, as shown.

9 Finish the spinosaurus by drawing its eye and pattern.

What Is a Stegosaurus?

Stegosauruses are known for having small heads, short necks, long rear legs, and two rows of bony **plates** along their backs. It is these plates that gave the stegosaurus its name. The word "stegosaurus" means "roof lizard" or "covered lizard" in Greek.

A stegosaurus was about the same size as a bus. It stood at 20 to 30 feet (6 to 9 m) long and could be up to 9 feet (2.75 m) tall at the hips. Stegosauruses weighed up to 2 tons (1,800 kg). As herbivores, they ate ferns and other leafy plants.

Tail
A stegosaurus's tail was strong and heavy. At the end of its tail were two pairs of sharp, pointed spikes called thagomizers. These spikes were used for protection from predators. They measured up to 4 feet (30 cm) long.

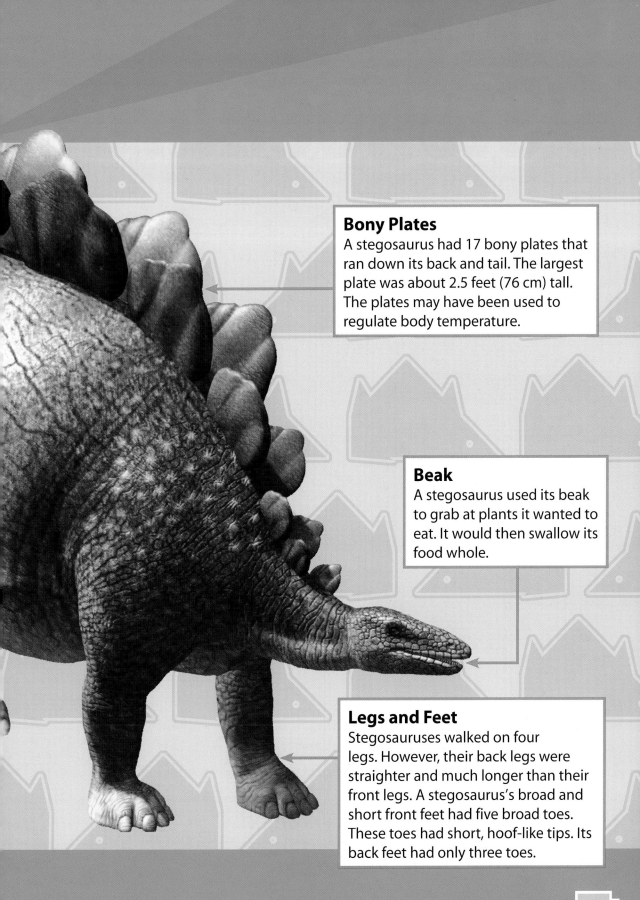

Bony Plates

A stegosaurus had 17 bony plates that ran down its back and tail. The largest plate was about 2.5 feet (76 cm) tall. The plates may have been used to regulate body temperature.

Beak

A stegosaurus used its beak to grab at plants it wanted to eat. It would then swallow its food whole.

Legs and Feet

Stegosauruses walked on four legs. However, their back legs were straighter and much longer than their front legs. A stegosaurus's broad and short front feet had five broad toes. These toes had short, hoof-like tips. Its back feet had only three toes.

How to Fold a
Stegosaurus

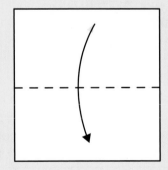

1 Fold in half, as shown.

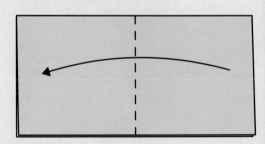

2 Fold in half, as shown.

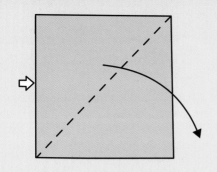

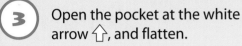

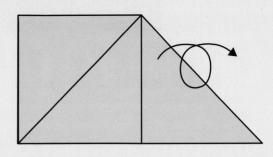

3 Open the pocket at the white arrow ⇧, and flatten.

4 Turn the paper over.

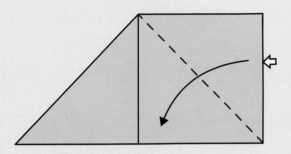

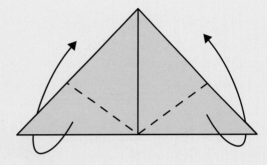

5 Open the pocket at the white arrow ⇧, and flatten.

6 Fold backward along the dotted lines.

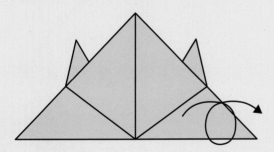

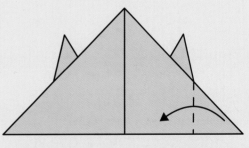

7 Turn the stegosaurus over.

8 To make the stegosaurus's tail, fold the right point in along the dotted line.

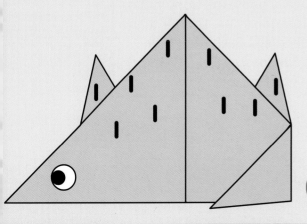

9 Finish the stegosaurus by drawing its eye and pattern.

What Is a Triceratops?

The word "triceratops" is Greek for "three-horned face." The triceratops was given this name because of the three horns it had on its head. Triceratopses were powerful dinosaurs. They could weigh up to 26,000 pounds (11,800 kg). An adult triceratops was about 30 feet (9 m) long and 10 feet (3 m) tall.

Triceratopses lived about 68 million years ago. They were herbivores that survived by eating shrubs and other plants. Due to their size, triceratopses could not move very quickly. Their top speed was only about 10 miles (16 km) per hour.

Legs and Feet
The triceratops had short, sturdy legs that helped support its heavy body. The front legs of a triceratops were shorter than its back legs. Each front foot had five toes, and each back foot had four toes.

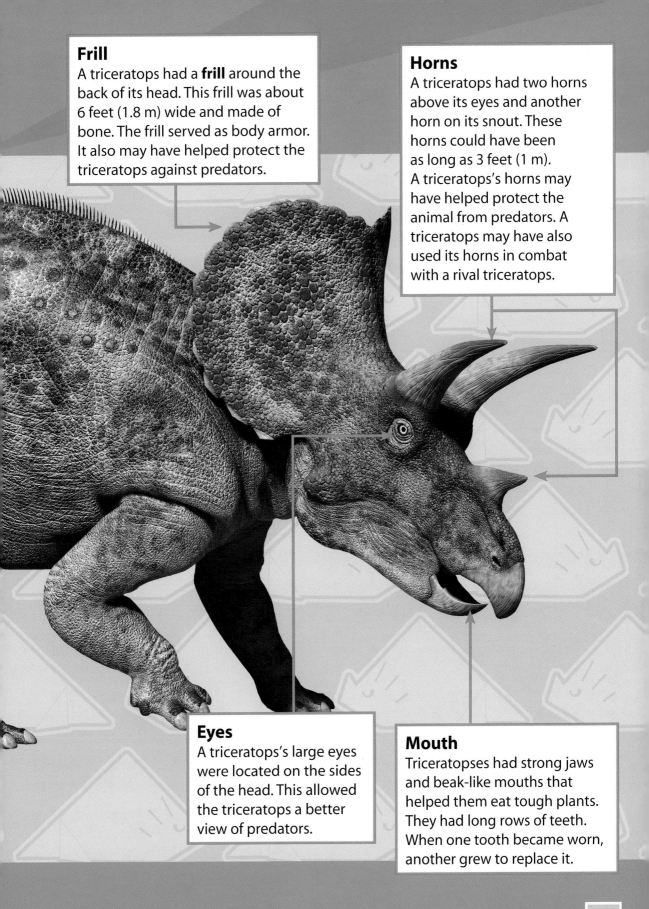

Frill
A triceratops had a **frill** around the back of its head. This frill was about 6 feet (1.8 m) wide and made of bone. The frill served as body armor. It also may have helped protect the triceratops against predators.

Horns
A triceratops had two horns above its eyes and another horn on its snout. These horns could have been as long as 3 feet (1 m). A triceratops's horns may have helped protect the animal from predators. A triceratops may have also used its horns in combat with a rival triceratops.

Eyes
A triceratops's large eyes were located on the sides of the head. This allowed the triceratops a better view of predators.

Mouth
Triceratopses had strong jaws and beak-like mouths that helped them eat tough plants. They had long rows of teeth. When one tooth became worn, another grew to replace it.

How to Fold a
Triceratops

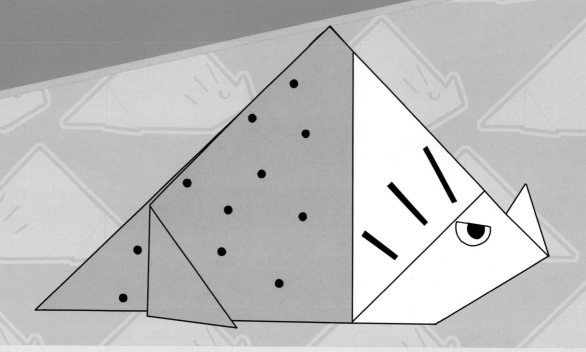

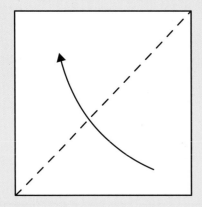

1 Fold in half along the dotted line, and crease.

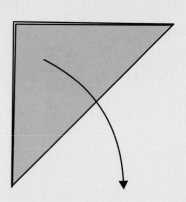

2 Open the paper.

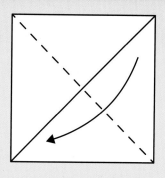

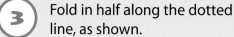

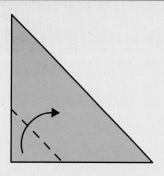

3 Fold in half along the dotted line, as shown.

4 Fold the top flap up along the dotted line, as shown.

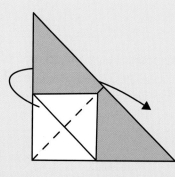

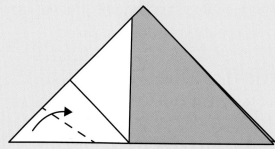

5 Fold backward along the dotted line, as shown.

6 To make the triceratops's horn, fold the left point in along the dotted line, as shown.

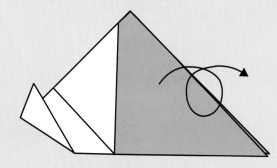

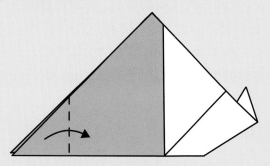

7 Turn the triceratops over.

8 To make the triceratops's tail, fold the left point in along the dotted line.

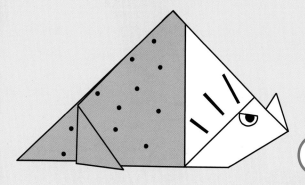

9 Finish the triceratops by drawing its eye and pattern.

What Is a
Tyrannosaurus Rex?

One of the best-known dinosaurs is the Tyrannosaurus rex. Often called the T. rex, the Tyrannosaurus was one of the largest carnivorous dinosaurs. A T. rex measured 40 feet (12 m) long and stood 15 to 20 feet (4.6 to 6 m) high. It could weigh up to 9 tons (8,165 kg).

The name is Greek for "king of the tyrant lizards." These dinosaurs were known to be fierce hunters. They would use their bone-crushing strength to attack other dinosaurs. T. rexes often fought one another, and at times might have even eaten each other.

Tail
A T. rex's tail was pointed and stiff. The tail helped the T. rex keep its balance. This allowed the T. rex to make fast turns when running.

Legs and Feet
T. rexes had strong legs. Each foot had three toes with very sharp claws. Unlike most other dinosaurs, T. rexes walked on their toes.

Skull

One of the most unique features of a T. rex was its huge skull. Measuring 5 feet (1.5 m) long, it protected the brain. Like the iguanodon, the T. rex's brain had a large area for processing odors. This meant the T. rex, like the iguanodon, used its sense of smell to find its prey.

Eyes

T. rexes had very large eyes. Each eye measured 3 inches (7.6 cm) in **diameter**. This is about the size of a softball. The eyes faced forward. This allowed the T. rex to judge distance, a helpful feature when hunting prey.

Jaw and Teeth

A T. rex's jaw measured up to 4 feet (1.2 m) long. Inside were about 60 **serrated** teeth. Some of these teeth were more than 8 inches (20 cm) long. With its powerful jaws and sharp teeth, a T. rex could eat 500 pounds (230 kg) of meat in a single bite.

Arms

T. rexes had short arms. At only 3 feet (1 m) long, these two-fingered arms could lift as much as 400 pounds (180 kg).

How to Fold a Tyrannosaurus Rex

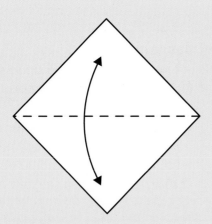

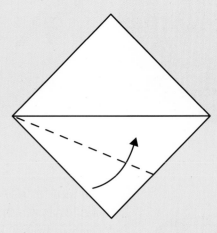

1. Fold in half, and crease. Open the paper.

2. Fold the bottom point up to meet the center line.

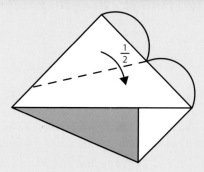

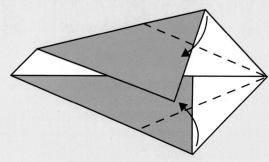

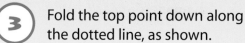

3 Fold the top point down along the dotted line, as shown.

4 Fold the top point in to meet the center line. Repeat along the bottom point.

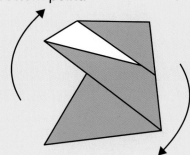

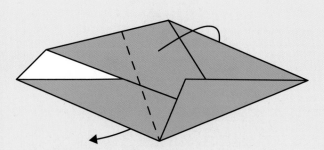

5 Fold backward along the dotted line, as shown.

6 Turn the T. rex.

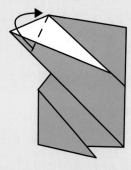

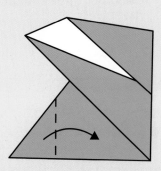

7 To make the T. rex's tail, fold the left point in along the dotted line.

8 To make the T. rex's mouth, fold backward along the dotted line.

9 Finish the T. rex by drawing its eye, teeth, and pattern.

Test Your Knowledge of Dinosaurs

1. Where were a brachiosaurus's nostrils located?

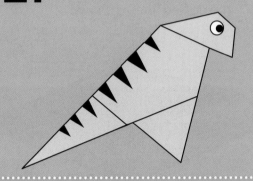

Answer: On a dome-shaped ridge on top of its head

2. What does the name "iguanodon" mean?

Answer: "Iguana tooth"

3. Where did the spinosaurus live?

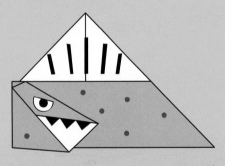

Answer: In swamps and marshes

4. How many bony plates did a stegosaurus have on its back and tail?

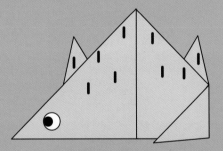

Answer: 17

5. What was a triceratops's frill made of?

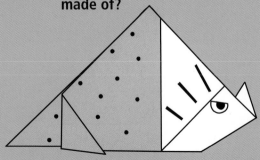

Answer: Bone

6. How much meat could a T. rex eat in a single bite?

Answer: 500 pounds (230 kg)

Want to learn more? Log on to www.av2books.com to access more content.

Make a Fossil

Materials
- Small natural object (shell, leaf, bone)
- Petroleum jelly
- Plaster of Paris
- Water
- Disposable plastic container

Steps
1. Choose an object found in nature, such as a bone or leaf, to create your own fossil.
2. Coat the object in petroleum jelly.
3. Mix some plaster of Paris together with water in a plastic container. Let it sit for a few minutes.
4. Press your object into the plaster of Paris, and leave it to dry.
5. When the plaster of Paris is totally dry, remove the object. The plaster of Paris will have the shape of your object embedded in it. This is your fossil.

Key Words

balance: a steady, secure position

body temperature: the level of heat the body makes

carnivorous: meat-eating

crest: a ridge on the top of an animal's head

diameter: the length of a straight line passing through the center of a circle

environment: the air, water, soil, and all other things that surround a person, animal, or plant

extinct: no longer living on Earth

fossils: the hardened remains of animals or plants that lived long ago

frill: a ruff of hair, feathers, skin, or bone around the neck of an animal

herbivores: animals that eat only plants

mates: the males or females of animal pairs

plates: flat structures that cover some animals

predators: animals that hunt other animals for food

prey: animals that are hunted as food

serrated: having a notched edge

species: animals or plants that share certain features

spikes: sharp, pointed pieces that stick out

spines: hard, pointed structures on an animal

Log on to www.av2books.com

AV² by Weigl brings you media enhanced books that support active learning. Go to www.av2books.com, and enter the special code found on page 2 of this book. You will gain access to enriched and enhanced content that supplements and complements this book. Content includes video, audio, weblinks, quizzes, a slide show, and activities.

AV² Online Navigation

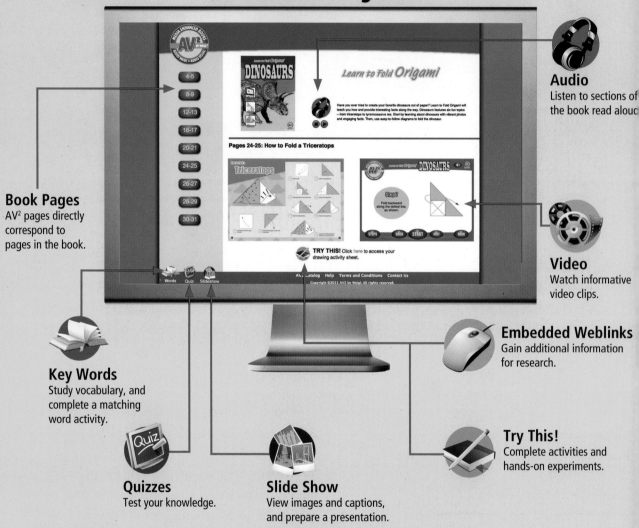

Audio
Listen to sections of the book read aloud

Video
Watch informative video clips.

Book Pages
AV² pages directly correspond to pages in the book.

Key Words
Study vocabulary, and complete a matching word activity.

Quizzes
Test your knowledge.

Slide Show
View images and captions, and prepare a presentation.

Embedded Weblinks
Gain additional information for research.

Try This!
Complete activities and hands-on experiments.

AV² was built to bridge the gap between print and digital. We encourage you to tell us what you like and what you want to see in the future.

Sign up to be an AV² Ambassador at www.av2books.com/ambassador.